Organization of Marriage Ministries

Marriage
Ministries

Organization of Marriage Ministries

Original title in Spanish: Organización del Ministerio para Matrimonios

Copyright © 2019 for the Church of the Nazarene
SAM Productions
Casilla de Correo 154, Código Postal 1629
Pilar, Buenos Aires, Argentina.

Authors: Patricia & Germán Picavea
Patricia Picavea, Spanish Editor
Mery Asenjo, Spanish Coeditor
Loysbel Pérez, Theology review

Disciples In Ministry is an editorial project of the Regional Office of the Church of the Nazarene in South America

Organization of Marriage Ministries in English is published by:
Mesoamerica Region Nazarene Discipleship International (NDI)
www.Discipleship.MesoamericaRegion.org
www.NdiResources.MesoamericaRegion.org

Translated into English from Spanish by: Bethany Cyr

Copyright © 2022 All rights reserved.
ISBN: 978-1-63580-319-8

Design by Slater Designer

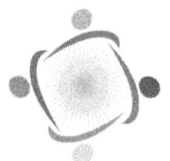

NAZARENE DISCIPLESHIP
INTERNATIONAL
MESOAMERICA REGION

Contents

Presentation

The DISCIPLES IN MINISTRY series of self-study courses is designed for disciples of the Lord Jesus Christ who are intentionally willing to fulfill His command to "make disciples of all nations" (Matthew 28:20).

Disciples are followers of their teacher. In the case of Christ's disciples, we not only follow our Master, we also want to be like Him. We really can't even imitate Him. Christian discipleship is allowing Jesus to be the owner, the master and the Lord of all that we are. That is to say, he has total control of our lives. When Christ Jesus is in absolute control, then He will begin to "be and do" in us, even more than we could "be and do" on our own. This radical concept of discipleship is for life.

Like any process, discipleship has its stages. The first is to receive Jesus as Savior and Lord, and to learn this means giving up our will until we reach the special moment when Jesus takes full control of every aspect of our lives. At that moment, "it is God who works in you to will and to act in order to fulfill his good purpose" (Philippians 2:13) in us. Without God's complete control, we cannot serve Him. Only after "being" can we move on to the stage of "doing."

The apostle Paul tells us that "we are God's handiwork, created in Christ Jesus to do good works, which God prepared in advance for us to do" (Ephesians 2:10). Now that we are part of the Body of Christ (the Church), and Jesus as the head controls us, we must find out how we can be of greater use to the body. The second part of discipleship is perfecting ourselves "for works of service, so that the body of Christ may be built up" (Ephesians 4:12).

These self-study notebooks will help us specialize in the call to serve Jesus Christ that God has designed for each of us. Now we are "a chosen people, a royal priesthood, a holy nation, God's special possession, that you may declare the praises of him who called you out of darkness into his wonderful light" (1 Peter 2:9). One of the best ways to announce the virtues of Jesus is by demonstrating who He is through a ministry in our local church, that is, by being an active part of his body.

This Disciples in Ministry program is comprised of six general courses and nine specialized courses in each specific ministry. The first six courses will guide us through the basic steps of discipleship: (1) Who is Jesus and what does it mean to follow him? (2) What does it mean to be in Christ? (3) What does it mean to be part of God's people? (4) What does it mean to grow in the likeness of Christ? (5) What does it mean to be a leader? (6) What does it mean to be a servant leader? The remaining nine courses will offer us specialized content in different ministries such as "Evangelism", "Lay Pastor", "Sunday School and Discipleship Ministries", "Communications", "Compassionate Ministries", "Youth", "Women", "Missions" and "Marriage".

Our prayer is that you will find your role in the "Body of Christ" and that this series of courses will help you become a disciple involved in ministry. For this reason God saved you and now you are part of the Body of Christ.

Dr. Christian Sarmiento
REGIONAL DIRECTOR
Church of the Nazarene
South America

The material you have in your hands is part of one of the courses of the Disciples in Ministry Project (DIM) that seeks "to equip the saints, to do the work of ministry" as established by the Word of God in Ephesians chapter 4 verse 12 (ISV).

This material has been prepared by different authors in order to provide you with a self-teaching resource to develop with excellence the ministry that the Lord has called you to carry out in his local church.

In no way is this material intended to replace a formal academic preparation for people whom God has called to fully dedicate their lives to ministry, because for this there are several institutions of theological education in the different countries of our Region.

How to use this material:

This course is divided into eight lessons, to be studied either individually or in groups. If it is possible to study the lessons in small groups, we believe it will be of much greater benefit.

The material is designed for self-study and does not necessarily require a teacher; however, if a pastor or knowledgeable leader of your local church can help you, we are sure that such help will be very useful.

You can decide the best times to study each lesson. The method can vary, and we hope that the lessons adjust to your schedule availability. We recommend that you study at least one lesson per week.

Before starting each lesson, please take into account the following:

- Spend time in prayer before you begin your study.

- Have a Bible handy so you can refer to the references given in each of the lessons.

- We recommend that you do one lesson at a time, taking the time to answer the questions raised, doing the proposed activities, and meeting the established objectives.

In each lesson you will find different sections identified with their respective icons. Below we explain what each of these sections means.

OBJECTIVES: The objectives are the goals that you will meet by the end of the lesson. We recommend that you read them and at the end of the lesson ask yourself if they have been met. These objectives are aimed at directing your values, your convictions as a believer, as well as knowing what you need to fulfill your ministry.

MAIN IDEAS: In this section you will find a summary of the most important aspects of the lesson. What you read here is what will be developed in more detail throughout the content. We suggest, at the end of the lesson, to go back to the Main Ideas and reaffirm the central concepts that you learned.

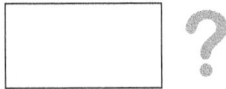

TEACHING HELPS: In the narrow columns of each lesson you will find some instructions related to the topic that is being developed. In most cases they are questions or observations that will help you understand and dialogue about the contents.

SUPPLEMENTARY NOTES: These are notes with additional information that will allow you to delve into the content you are studying.

Why today do we observe Sunday and not Saturday as the day of the Lord in our churches?

1. Biblical Evidence
Acts 20:7 says: "On the first day of the week we came together to break bread".

2. Evidence from the "Fathers" of the Church:
St. Ignatius of Antioch (AD 107) said: "Those who walked in ancient practices attained unto newness of hope, no longer keeping Sabbaths, but according to the Lord's way of life ..."

ACTIVITIES: At the end of each lesson you will find an exercise that will reinforce what you have learned through questions, activities or practical instruction. We suggest you dedicate the time necessary to complete each activity, which will allow you to self-assess your learning.

We encourage you to continue in your spiritual development as a leader of the church of Jesus Christ. God has reserved for you a wonderful ministry in his local church and we hope that this course will guide and instruct you to fulfill this sacred task.

Why Marriage Ministry?

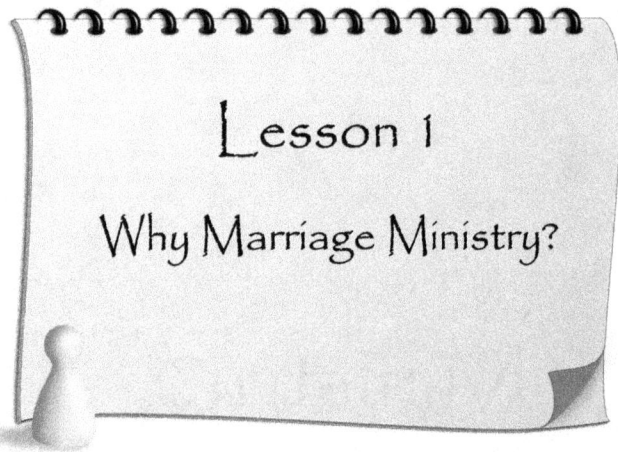

Lesson 1

Why Marriage Ministry?

OBJECTIVES

- Be aware of the generalities of today's marriage situations.

- Understand the importance of marriage ministry in the local church.

- Know the reason for Marriage Ministries.

MAIN IDEAS

- In local churches there is an urgent need to develop marriage ministry from a pastoral perspective.

- In the local church it is important to develop a marriage ministry that promotes the development and growth of happy married couples.

The Current State of Marriage

It is with great concern that we share our firm conviction that the institution of marriage is about to descend into a state of turmoil like no other time in human history. The enemy is attacking marriage from different angles, with the ultimate goal being to destroy it completely.

Marriage researchers have been warning of the threatening storm to which marriage is being subjected, a situation that is increasing exponentially. Two sociologists, David Popenoe and Barbara Dafoe Whitehead of Rutgers University in New Jersey, USA, conducted a study of the family between 1960 and 1999, and concluded that the institution of marriage seems to be dying.[1] Today, simply by looking at reality, we have ample and convincing evidence about the accuracy of their conclusions based on almost four decades of research. The situation of decline in marriage and the naturalization that it's currently experiencing is such that in Uruguay, CEPAL warned that a culture of divorce has been established in that country.[2]

We could assume that this serious situation that marriage is experiencing does not concern Christian marriages. But when we look inside the Christian church, we discover that the marriages within the Christian faith are influenced by the enemy and suffer the same fatal consequences as those who do not live under the lordship of Christ and the values of the Kingdom. Some years ago, a 1996 investigation by Christian researcher George Barna revealed that the percentage of married and divorced Christians was higher (27%) than the percentage of non-Christians in the same situation (23%).[4] And in Brazil, a survey revealed that 40% of women who say they are victims of physical and verbal abuse by their husbands are evangelicals.[5]

The Importance Of Marriage Ministry In The Local Church

> In Ecuador, between 2006 and 2016, marriages decreased by 22.01% and divorces increased by 83.45%.[3]

Given the reality that's been described, it seems that very few churches are providing adequate pastoral care for the marriages in their local congregations, in ways that address the situations that marriages are experiencing today.

As the Church of the Nazarene on the South America Region we are aware of the current situation and understand the value of this relationship that was designed and established by God in the development of the family, church, and society. Therefore, we are determined to serve with passion in an effort to rescue and re-unite marriages, as well as develop a ministry for married couples that emphasizes the growth and strengthening of this central nucleus of society. Nazarene Discipleship International (NDI), under the department of Ministry to Adults,[6] is called to serve in this specific area in a clear and urgent way. Without border and cultural limits, with adequate and pertinent contextualization, it is expected that Marriage Ministries will be an integral part of the active ministries in each local congregation.

Through Marriage Ministries we propose a way to respond to this need through the local church and with a pastoral perspective. Through these modules, we will share the purpose, the objectives, the needs, the materials and different resources and ideas that we hope will be a guide and will help to carry out this ministry.

> We encourage the entire church to take up the challenge of working to strengthen marriages, being useful instruments, guided by God to proclaim the biblical truth about the institution of marriage.

Based on your context, in what ways does the enemy attack marriages?

9

Let's take the challenge, and with God's help let's work to develop this ministry in every local church. In this way we will help provide growth and development to the wonderful and irreplaceable institution created by God called marriage.

Why Marriage Ministries?

Marriage Ministries was started from observing the reality of marriages in general and how the Christian church approaches marriage in particular. We cannot help but admit that the problems within marriages grow day by day without being resolved and, in many cases, bring the marriage to the point of separation and divorce. What do we do?! This is the cry and the obligatory question of those of us who are involved in pastoral work and committed to God in carrying out his mission.

By reading the Bible we can conclude that happiness was part of God's plan for marriage from the beginning, because in the bond of marriage there were principles of enjoyment, companionship and procreation. "The Lord God said, 'It is not good for the man to be alone. I will make a helper suitable for him'" Genesis 2:18. In fact, when God presents Eve to Adam (v.22), Adam displays a certain happiness and astonishing admiration for God's creation (v.23). His entire statement refers to the similarity and complementarity they will share living a life together. The Creator's conclusion after he blesses them both and charges them with the work they were to do helps us see the full picture: "...it was very good" Genesis 1:31. This is an expression of happiness that refers to satisfaction and pleasure from God.

> "So God created mankind in his own image, in the image of God he created them; male and female he created them."
> Genesis 1:27

"So God created mankind in his own image, in the image of God he created them; male and female he created them" Genesis 1:27. We can say that marriage is an institution that was born from the very heart of God. It was not a random act, but he desired it (James 1:18). So, in no way can we think that marriage was a social creation, a fad or a casual result of the existence of two beings. The marriage bond was intended by God from the very creation of the human being. "That is why a man leaves his father

> Do you believe that happiness in marriage was part of God's original plan?

and mother and is united to his wife, and they become one flesh." Genesis 2:24. We consider marriage to be a sacred institution that we must guard against the attacks of the enemy, who has been trying to destroy it from the beginning (Genesis 3). God's idea from the beginning was that together, a man and a woman, would live happily married, in companionship and harmony, forming the basic unit of humanity (Genesis 12:3). In the divine plan for marriage we find all the resources to make a man and a woman two completely fulfilled beings, in other words: a happily married couple.

> The Creator's conclusion after He blesses them both and charges them with the work they were to do helps us see the bigger picture: "...and it was very good" Genesis 1:31.

In the most extensive (beginning in 1938) and largest study ever conducted on the factors that influence people's true happiness, "researchers found that marital satisfaction has a protective effect on people's mental health. ...People in their 80's who had happy marriages reported that their moods didn't suffer even on days when they had the most physical pain. Those in unhappy marriages felt emotional as well as physical pain".[7]

Today we have an urgent need to develop in our local churches a permanent, dedicated ministry for marriages from a pastoral perspective. We must turn our eyes to the principles for marriage that God established in his Word, make them a reality in our lives and promote them so that every day there are more and more happily married couples in our churches.

> In our local churches today we have an urgent need to develop a ministry for married couples.

11

Instructions

Do you think it's important to provide a ministry to married couples in the church? Why or why not?

_____

_____

_____

_____

Do you think that Marriage Ministries is a good option to meet the need to minister to married couples? Why?

_____

_____

_____

_____

If you think that Marriage Ministries would be a good option, what will be your first step?

_____

_____

_____

_____

Purpose and Objectives of Marriage Ministry

Lesson 2

Purpose and Objectives of Marriage Ministry

OBJECTIVES

- To see marriage as a unit made up of two people with very different but complementary personalities and characteristics.

- Recognize that marriages need to grow and develop integrally.

- Know the objectives that are pursued through Marriage Ministries which are divided into five areas: spiritual, emotional, social, physical and mental.

MAIN IDEAS

- There is an urgent need in the local church to create space for marriages to grow.

- It is important to develop a comprehensive marriage ministry that aims to strengthen the different areas of being human and of marriage.

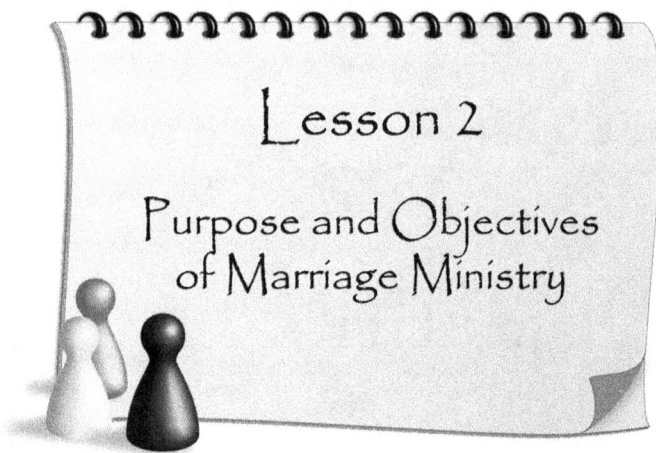

We Are Whole Beings

It is important to keep in mind that we are whole beings. As such we need to pay attention to all areas of our being (spiritual, emotional, social, physical and mental) since they're all important and affect our lives, individual and married.

Quite often there is a natural tendency in the church to put more emphasis and work on the spiritual area and, often without any conscious intention, neglect the development of the other areas. On other occasions, however, the needs that correspond to the emotional area of the spouses are spiritualized and therefore the real needs of the couple are not reached.

With regard to the whole being, the definition of health used by WHO is as follows: "Health is a state of complete physical, mental and social well-being, and not merely the absence of infirmities or diseases".[1]

Today in different branches of human activity, the concept of being whole is being understood better and better, and interdisciplinary work is being undertaken to provide a more effective response to the different problems that affect us. For example, in the health field this is becoming more evident every day, where it is being observed that, "a reaction such as great stress can imply a drop in the function of the immune system, or an illness, serious or not so serious, may imply a psycho-pathological condition, such as depression".[2]

In this sense, God, in his Word, lets us see that we are whole beings. In Mark 12:30-31, Jesus says, "'Love the Lord your God with all your heart and with all your soul and with all your mind and with all your strength.' The second is this: 'Love your neighbor as yourself.' There is no commandment greater than these". Jesus makes it clear to his listeners that God requires love to be an action and that it must come from the whole person, so Jesus highlights each of the areas of the person: heart = emotional, soul = spiritual, mind = mental, strength = physical, and neighbor = social. Jesus was responding to a question asked by people with a marked inclination to study the Scriptures (mental) but who often neglected love for their neighbor (social).

In the Bible there are countless references to the whole of the human being, to the connection between the mental, emotional, and physical, between the tangible and the intangible. In Psalm 32:3-4, the psalmist David says, "When I kept silent, my bones wasted away ... my strength was sapped as in the heat of summer." David is referring to unconfessed sin that, while he kept it hidden in the depths of his being, was greatly affecting his physical health.

> Human beings are a complete unit made up of different areas. One area cannot be left out or developed more than another.

It's very clear that we need to develop each area of the human being. Human beings are a complete unit made up of different areas. One area cannot be left out or developed more than another. In addition, when two people establish a marriage, they must take into account that the areas of each spouse may not only have different levels of development but they must also be linked to the marriage relationship.

From ministry to marriages, we need to develop a comprehensive approach to the different areas of the human being, and constantly keep in mind that there are many factors at play in the growth and development of a marriage. So we cannot delve only into the spiritual area; we must help couples see the different areas that interact and need to be worked on.

It's very likely that in order to adequately attend to this approach, we will need the expertise of different people who are knowledgeable about the issues of the previously mentioned areas.

What do you think about the wholeness of the human being?

General Purpose of the Ministry

"Create a space (time and place) where married couples have time to grow, develop, enjoy, learn and share together what God has for them."

Why is creating space so important? Let's look for a moment at the reality of a typical local church. In it, children have their space, young people have their space, women have their space, and marriages? The answer is most likely no. Normally marriages do not have a space on the church meeting calendar. They are absent when it comes to overall church planning in the minds of those who do the planning.

So, let's start by creating space for marriages. Let's make exclusive space for them in the general planning of the church. In this space let's cover as many important aspects as possible so that marriages are truly shepherded and people feel supported and accompanied in their relationship.

Specific Objectives

Below are the specific objectives in each of the five areas of a human life, with the purpose of maintaining a comprehensive approach in the pastoral care of married couples. In no way is it intended to be a complete list, rather it is hoped that these objectives will be contextualized and improved in order to achieve greater effectiveness in the Marriage Ministry of your local church.

Spiritual Area

Of course, this is the foundation for life (John 10:10) and we must ensure that the spiritual area is properly addressed, but since it is the area of greatest emphasis within the church, it may be a temptation for the coordinators to spend a majority of their time on it without touching on the other areas. We must try to maintain an equal balance with the other areas. For this we propose the following objectives:

1. To facilitate spiritual growth within the marriage. Conduct Bible studies, devotionals, and reflections that teach biblical truths that are practical for married life.

2. To help couples find God's plan for their lives. This can be accomplished by discovering God's purpose for marriage in

Why is it important to have a space for married couples?

His original plan, and by going deeper into the redemption in Christ and discovering how it affects marriage.

3. To bring spouses who do not know Christ closer to Him. Understand that the fulfillment of the Great Commission (Matthew 28:19-20) must also reach marriages, integrating the non-Christian spouse through activities and relationships that create bonds that facilitate an encounter with the Lord.

Emotional Area

This is an area that we all need to work on in our lives. When it comes to marriage, the emotional area is vital. God created us with emotions and the Bible gives us many accounts of this. The Bible speaks of emotions such as joy (Psalm 30:11; Proverbs 5:18), resentment (Hebrews 12:15), anger (Proverbs 15:1), love (Mark 12:30-31) and fear (Luke 12:7) among many more that are present in our lives and marriages. We must know our emotions, distinguish what they are and how they affect us, and learn to manage them.

For the emotional area we suggest the following objectives:

1. To provide resources and information to married couples so they can work on their marriage relationship from the emotional aspect.

2. To provide helpful tools for the different stages of crisis that marriages face (birth of the first child, job loss, moving to a different house or to a different country, death of a child, etc.).

3. To provide Pastoral support and guidance to married couples as they go through the processes of emotional healing.

Social Area

In the Word of God we see that fellowship or "koinonia" was an important aspect from the very beginning of Jesus' ministry. His ministry was eminently relational, all the time Jesus was surrounded by people and He Himself wanted to be with people. He ate with the people (Mark 2:16), traveled to be with people (John 4), visited people in their homes (Luke 19:1-10) and even cooked a farewell meal (John 21:1-14). His followers

17

continued to do all of these things after his ascension and as part of the dynamic of a living church (Acts 2:46-47).

> "When they landed, they saw a fire of burning coals there with fish on it, and some bread. Jesus said to them, 'Bring some of the fish you have just caught.' So Simon Peter climbed back into the boat and dragged the net ashore... Jesus said to them, 'Come and have breakfast.' ...Jesus came, took the bread and gave it to them, and did the same with the fish." John 21:9-13

In our culture, social interaction is very important, so we must provide time for social interaction and encourage it to be naturally incorporated into the lives of new converts. Of course, it's always important to maintain a balance, since social activities can get out of hand. To promote social interaction we propose the following objectives:

1. To help with the development of social interaction within marriage by creating space and time for couples to share.

2. To create a space where married couples can share with other married couples their experiences in an atmosphere of trust and confidentiality.

3. To establish connections with married couples who do not know Christ so that they have the opportunity to come to Christ.

Physical Area

Beyond chasing fashion or going along with the current trend of body worship, we need to be all about caring for the body as a creation of God (Genesis 2:7) and a temple of the Holy Spirit (1 Corinthians 6:19). Unfortunately health care is not usually a priority, and in many cases this leads to various problems in the marriage relationship. In this area we suggest the following objectives:

1. To make the married couples aware that caring for the body is important and we need to care for the health of our spouse as well. This may include encouraging them to have regular medical check-ups and to have an appropriate diet.

2. To create space so that the married couples learn to enjoy and take part in physical activity, exercising, taking walks or a sport of some kind.

3. To provide adequate nutritional information according to the different needs of the married couples.

Mental Area

The mental area must be developed like all the others, but we need to work intentionally to encourage mental development since we face basic problems such as a lack of interest in reading. This means that married couples do not seek self-training but instead rely on information that others tell them. Curiously, God in his Word draws our attention to this by saying: "Do not be like the horse or the mule, which have no understanding but must be controlled by bit and bridle or they will not come to you" Psalm 32:9. The idea here is that we are not horses or mules, we have understanding like the Creator and we must use it.

Married couples must be guided to develop themselves intellectually so they can respond better to the daily challenges of their married life. In this area, we propose the following objectives:

1. To provide adequate information for a married couple to experience a marriage that is fulfilling.

2. To renew the way we think about marriage by bridging the universal and transcendent principles of God with each particular culture and its own styles of marriage.

3. To help incorporate God's biblical principles for marriage into daily life.

Which of these areas do you think is the most neglected? Why?

19

Instructions

Why do we say that we are "whole" beings?

_____

_____

Keeping in mind that we are "whole" beings and that there are different areas that we must develop, write an activity that will strengthen each area to help develop the whole person.

_____

_____

_____

Spiritual: _____

_____

_____

Emotional: _____

_____

_____

Social: _____

_____

_____

Physical: _____

_____

_____

Mental: _____

_____

_____

Ministry Leaders

Lesson 3

Ministry Leaders

OBJECTIVES

- Know the characteristics that are necessary for the coordinators of Marriage Ministries to have.

- Have a general idea of the functions that the coordinators of Marriage Ministries will carry out.

MAIN IDEA

- It is important to carefully consider the people who will be in charge of Marriage Ministries and to make sure that they know what their responsibilities will be.

This is a very important aspect for the development of the ministry. It should not be taken lightly and neither should it be exaggerated. It's as bad to think that anyone can run this ministry as it is to think that we'll never find the right people to do it. Both extremes are bad and can make it fail before it starts.

Marriage ministry coordinators, first and foremost, should be a couple that has a strong marriage.[1] This couple will be visible to those they minister to all of the time. They will be a reference for other married couples and an example for young people who are thinking about marriage. The purpose of the Marriage Ministry Coordinators is not to be social coordinators that organize activities throughout the year, but to be people who are capable of facing this responsibility with hearts that want to help marriages heal and grow. For this reason, and with all this in mind, it is necessary to take the following into consideration.

The selection of the coordinators of Marriage Ministries in the local church is a very important aspect of its development. It should not be taken lightly nor should it be exaggerated.

22

Prayer: It's normal that the desire of our hearts is to help where we see a need. Due to the urgency of the need we hurry to implement a ministry that helps meet that need, but we neglect a fundamental first step in the search for workers: prayer. Jesus warned us that there would be a lack of workers for the task but also told us where to go to find them: "Ask the Lord of the harvest, ..., to send out workers..." Luke 10:2. It's a very clear principle: every ministry must begin with a prayerful search. The Lord will guide us to the right people to carry out the important task of ministering to married couples. However, that does not mean that the work is finished. We will need to share with them, teach them, shepherd them and serve together with them, just as Jesus taught us (Luke 6:12-20).

> The Lord will guide us to the right people to carry out the important task of ministering to married couples.

Marriage: It's essential that this task be coordinated by a married couple. The nature of the ministry requires it. It can cause a big problem if a single person, male or female, tries to run Marriage Ministries. We must also be sure that it's a married couple that is married legally, civilly and religiously. If necessary, we must request the documents that prove it. If they are people who have transferred from another church or denomination, we can speak with the pastor or the relevant authorities to be sure of their situation. It would be frustrating and could be damaging to discover, after the ministry coordinators have been leading for awhile, an unusual situation that affects the integrity of Marriage Ministries.

On the other hand, having a married couple as coordinators provides a balance in the approach to the different problems that concern the marriage. This isn't a minor matter, since sometimes marriage ministries tend to have a bias in their treatment of the issues. By having a married couple as leaders, a healthy balance can be achieved as we have both a male and a female perspective in matters that require it.

Members of the local church: As we said before, the coordinating couple of Marriage Ministries will be a model for the congregation all of the time. Like it or not, for many people they will be the reference when it comes to marriage. For this reason, it's important that the coordinating couple be members in good standing of the local church where the ministry takes place. This means that they must be people with an obvious commitment to the Lord and who are active in the local church. It's understood that they will be knowledgeable in the doctrine of the Church of the Nazarene and committed to it. (See the Manual of the Church of the Nazarene 2017-2021, page 26-36; The Covenant of Christian Conduct, page 46-61).

> The coordinating couple must be members in good standing of the local church and with an obvious commitment to the Lord shown by their involvement and commitment to their local church.

Good Christian Reputation: A good testimony or reputation is a requirement of every Christian and becomes essential when we take on a leadership position. It's not about being a "good person" or being well liked, but about people who –and in this case a married couple who– embodies the principles and values of the Word of God and puts them into practice in their daily lives. We do not mean that this couple should have a perfect marriage, like a "finished product", free of conflicts. Instead we are referring to a couple that keeps Christ at the center of their lives and their relationship, that lives married life from a biblical perspective and that makes use of Bible-based resources to face the different situations that arise.

Inspiring Married Life: We are talking about people who spread their joy of sharing their lives in marriage. Not a perfect marriage, but one that, in the midst of the different circumstances that they have to live, model lives that reflect God's purpose for marriage. A marriage that inspires others to follow their example. In addition, we can point out the following aspects to take into account:

Responsible: The coordinating couple must be responsible for the commitments they make. The dates, times, and places announced for activities must be respected at all times, because constant changes produce instability in the ministry and it loses credibility.

Constant Preparation. The married couple that assumes this ministry must be in ongoing training. This can be informal: attending conferences, workshops, short courses; formal: pursuing careers related to the ministry; or personal: constantly reading and studying books, documents and different materials related to the theme of marriages and its biblical and theological aspects. Times change and with them many things are changing in relation to marriages. The couple that leads this ministry must be aware of this and constantly be trying to be up to date with the changes and new currents of thought that are emerging.

Work as a team. It's crucial that the coordinators of Marriage Ministries are willing to work as a team, since the many tasks that the ministry entails cannot be adequately carried out alone. They must involve other couples that can contribute their different talents and experiences to enrich the ministry and carry out the different tasks that the ministry requires. This is an important aspect to ensure the life, development and continuity of the ministry. In this team, the future leaders of the ministry will be trained.

Job Description

Every person who is called to serve in a ministry must know what is expected of him and his service to God and the church. For this reason, the couple that is selected to coordinate Marriage Ministries needs to have a description, as clear as possible, of the functions that correspond to them and that they will be expected to carry out.

We suggest that this job description be shared when speaking with the couple that the Lord has led to be invited to coordinate the ministry. By speaking with the couple and presenting the job description, you are giving them the opportunity to learn exactly what is expected of them as coordinators of Marriage Ministries. This will help them make a better decision before the Lord.

> The couple that is asked to coordinate Marriage Ministries needs to have a clear description of the functions that correspond to them and that they will need to develop.

Below are job descriptions for local and district coordinating couples:

How do you think these characteristics impact those serving in Marriage Ministries?

25

Marriage Ministries
Job Description

Responsibility: Local Coordinators

Area of Responsibility: The Local Church

Period of Service: We suggest a 2 year commitment with the possibility of 2 more years, based on their annual reviews.

Reports: In writing, to the NDI Council or local NDI board.[2]

The Marriage Ministries Local Coordinator couple is expected to be a couple in good standing who is actively involved in the local church. They must serve on and be accountable to the NDI Council.[1]

The Coordinating Couple Must:

1. Determine the needs and interests of the couples in the local congregation, through observation, study and any other way possible.

2. Present a ministry plan with its respective budget and inform the local NDI Adult Council or local NDI board.

3. Provide a space where married couples have time to grow, develop, enjoy, learn and share together what God has for them.

4. Promote and publicize wedding activities in every way possible.

5. Identify areas of need within the church and community where Marriage Ministries can serve.

6. Provide Bible studies, prayer groups, and other means to assist married couples in their spiritual development and growth.

7. Help couples develop and use their talents, gifts, and abilities.

8. Incorporate Marriage Ministries into the overall church program.

9. Cooperate with district Marriage Ministries Coordinators, promote and participate in district Marriage Ministries activities.

10. Share ideas, concerns, and suggestions for ministry improvement with the District Marriage Ministries Coordinators.

IMPORTANT: Keep the pastor, NDI Adult Council or local NDI board informed of all communications.

Marriage Ministries
Job Description

Responsibility: District Coordinators

Area of Responsibility: The District

Period of Service: We suggest a 2 year commitment with the possibility of 2 more years, based on their annual reviews.

Reports: In writing, to the District NDI Council and the District NDI Convention.[2]

It is expected that the District Coordinators of Marriage Ministries are a couple in good standing, that participates in the District NDI Council, if there is one, or in its absence, on the District NDI Board and must be responsible to the same.[1]

The Coordinating Couple Must:

1. Develop a District Ministry Plan for Marriage Ministries.

2. Motivate, train and assist in the implementation of Marriage Ministries in each local church on your district.

3. Serve as advisors to the local Marriage Ministries coordinators.

4. Develop an administrative and operational structure on the district that allows the development and growth of Marriage Ministries.

5. Know extensively the materials available for Marriage Ministries on your region.

6. Share information received from the Region, the Field and the District with the local Coordinators of Marriage Ministries.

7. Create and keep up-to-date a Database of Marriage Ministries that exist in the Churches of the Nazarene on your district.

8. Create and keep up-to-date a Database of the different resources (Nazarene and others) related to different problems that exist within marriages, and if those resources are available on your district.

9. Share ideas, concerns, and suggestions for ministry improvement with the District NDI Council.

IMPORTANT: Keep the District NDI Council informed of all communications.

Instructions

Briefly detail what steps should be followed to select a couple to be the Coordinators of Marriage Ministries and what characteristics they should have?

_____
_____
_____
_____
_____

Write a possible ministry plan for one year including an estimated budget.

_____
_____
_____
_____
_____
_____
_____
_____
_____
_____
_____
_____
_____
_____
_____
_____

Premarital Courses

Lesson 4

Premarital Courses

OBJECTIVES

- Make sure the importance of developing a premarital course as part of Marriage Ministries in the local church is recognized.

- Know the different aspects that should be considered when implementing a premarital course.

MAIN IDEAS

- Premarital courses are an essential resource in the local church due to their importance in preparing a couple for married life.

- The topics to be discussed should explore all aspects of married life, from a biblical perspective and with absolute clarity.

- The premarital courses must be conducted in a timely manner so that they result in the greatest possible learning for the couple(s) preparing for marriage.

- Consider carefully who will be selected to teach the premarital courses and the responsibility that entails.

Why A Premarital Course?

When someone shows us their wedding photos, we are dazzled by everything we see, but we will never know everything that happened before that moment: the ceremony, the exchange of rings, the I do!, the kiss and the celebration.

Beginning with the marriage proposal, through the notification of the parents, relatives, and friends, the paperwork, organization of the ceremony and the honeymoon and until the day of the wedding, an infinity of things happen and a mountain of detailed logistics must be carried out.

But after all that happens, in the blink of an eye, the newlyweds find themselves facing a life together that will present endless challenges for which, many times, they have had no preparation. Because we, as Marriag Ministries Coordinators, are aware of this situation, we must come along side this process. While it's true that it's difficult to determine when people are ready for marriage, but we can guide and advise and shepherd the couple in the process. For these reasons we can see the validity of offering premarital courses that help couples understand their future life from the perspective of God's Word.

The importance of a premarital course lies in the fact that it will help the couple to see important aspects that will accompany them throughout their married life. The aspects discussed will help them face daily life as a married couple, and the challenges that they will encounter as a couple. If the premarital course is carried out conscientiously, it may well be the element of prevention for many situations that the couple will no longer have to resolve. It will also result in preparation to fully enjoy

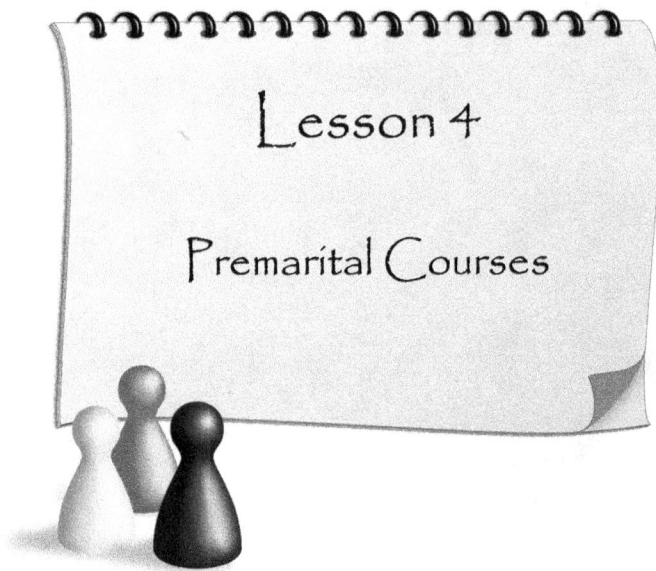

every moment of the daily life of their married life. In this regard, a survey conducted in the United States states: "the authors found that participation in premarital education was associated with higher levels of satisfaction and commitment in marriage and lower levels of conflict-and also reduced odds of divorce".[1]

Course Scope

Although all teaching has an immediate scope, it's important to understand that the scope of a premarital course in the medium and long term must be considered because the future life of the married couples

> The importance of a premarital course lies in the fact that it helps to see the important aspects of married life before the marriage commitment is made.

will count on it. Many dating couples take marriage lightly, as a formality or a prerequisite that they must meet. Regardless, this somewhat inadequate attitude prevents them from benefiting from all the richness that a premarital course can offer them.

On the other hand, other engaged couples take advantage of each lesson and as soon as they become aware of its importance, they incorporate it into their lives and (depending on the lesson) they put it into practice even during their courtship while they're taking the premarital course. One thing must be made clear; although they will never be "completely prepared" for marriage, they can learn fundamental aspects of married life and be guided by what they learn.

Topics to Consider in a Premarital Course

Although there are countless topics to deal with, it is important to cover some basic and fundamental topics for those who are beginning married life together. A premarital course is not couples counseling or therapy. Therefore, a premarital course will touch on general aspects without going into the particularities of each couple. However, the content and action of the Holy Spirit during the course can make each person feel mobilized to work on the aspects that require it in their lives, dating relationship, and future marriage.

Below, we present a list of topics we consider essential to be included in a premarital course:

Commitment: It's very valuable for the brides and grooms to understand the scope of the marriage commitment, and the value of their promise or vows that they will express to each other on the wedding day. It's very revealing, and sometimes even shocking, for the brides and grooms to work with the vows, read through them, listen to them and discover their implications.

> Although all teaching has an immediate scope, the scope of a premarital course in the medium and long term must be considered because future life of the married couples will depend on it.

Do you think that premarital courses are necessary? Why?

31

Another aspect of commitment is the reason(s) why the couple wants to get married. There are many reasons why people want to start a life together and formalize a marriage, but are they good reasons? Are they valid? Can the couple be wrong? All reasons deserve to be considered and analyzed in the light of the Word of God because it's essential that the couples understand that marriage is, above all things, a relationship of love and commitment for life.

Communication: Communication is essential in human life, in fact without it we die. Communication is an element that traverses through the entire married life. This must be understood by each individual and by the couple as the fundamental tool to help build a healthy marriage.

Effective communication is an indispensable tool in marriage. Effective communication contains basic aspects that each couple needs to know and learn to manage so that their marriages grow and develop in a healthy manner. Aspects such as active listening, empathy, verbal and nonverbal communication, construction of dialogue, assessment of what the other spouse said, good attitude, clarity and honesty cannot be missing from a premarital course. Equally important is letting the couples know that they will be the ones responsible for prioritizing and finding time to develop effective marital communication throughout their lives together.

Roles: When talking about roles, there is often a tendency to relate it to power, superiority, a hierarchy and authority, aspects that were not at all the ideals of the marriage relationship and that were never part of the plan of the Creator of marriage (Genesis 1:26-27; 2:24; 1:28-31). Cultural models, family and traditions have been adapted away from the biblical model, which brings frustration, pain and sadness to the lives of many people. Therefore, in a premarital course it is essential to reflect on the model for marriage that is established by the Word of God.

It will be helpful for the couple preparing for marriage to know that, in marriage, unity prevails over any individuality, that in Christ marriage has a new paradigm (Matthew 19:4-6), that marriage is a language of its own where the roles rotate and move around the needs and abilities of its members, that companionship, collaboration and solidarity must be constantly sought, and that common agreement of one with the other in love must never be lacking.

Finances: Financial problems are one of the main conflicts in marriages and have led to the ruin of many marriages. The issue of finances becomes difficult to deal with and on many occasions the spouses "resolve" it in ways that bring them resignation, bitterness and resentment.

Dealing with the issue of proper financial management is essential for those who want to share their lives in marriage. Finances should also speak to our faith in God and reflect the unity of marriage. How do we earn a living? How much do we give to God? What do we spend our money on and why? Do we save? Do we invest? It's essential that the premarital course advises and guides couples in

the preparation of a single budget, through mutual agreement, that although they are engaged, they can begin to follow knowing that in reality they will soon live as "one flesh".

Conflict: It's extremely important to help boyfriends, girlfriends, and newlyweds understand that a couple that loves each other has conflicts, it's that simple. After the wedding, regardless of how wonderful it was, marital conflicts will occur, because conflicts are part of human existence. They are universal and we must learn how to face them and solve them. The real secret lies in how we solve conflicts, not how we avoid them, because a life without conflicts is simply not possible.

It's important for couples to understand that conflicts exist between couples who love each other and stay married as well as between those who get divorced; the difference lies in the way each couple handled the conflict. It will also be very helpful for couples to know that there are no secret recipes to solving conflicts. Although there are limits or boundaries to respect, they are the ones who, through daily work on their relationship (with dedication and commitment), will discover how to face and solve each conflict.

Sex: When we talk about marriage we cannot leave out the topic of sex. Not because it is the only thing that matters, but because it is important. Sex is the radical difference between marriage and all other human relationships (Genesis 2:24).

In a premarital course we must include this topic and make clear to future spouses the fundamental aspects about sex that are reflected in the Word of God. We must demolish the myths that have been built around sex and that permanently damage God's original idea, taking the subject to the crude, dirty and vulgar. Although today it seems that much is said about this topic, reality tells us that every day we move further away from what God intended when he created sex. Repeatedly we listen to people who perceive sex as a duty to fulfill (on the part of women) or as a right to receive (on the part of men); others perceive it as a necessary evil, as an uncontrollable desire, as a need to be satisfied, or as a source of sin that brings anguish and pain to people. But as we look at what the Bible says, we find that sex within marriage is sacred, a way to share our love, for the purpose of mutual satisfaction and for reproduction. Sex is not only physical but is linked to all areas of our being. Sex results in a total and voluntary surrender between a man and a woman in the context of marriage.

Spiritual Life: God's place in this new relationship should definitely be covered in a premarital course. Many people get married and a new routine envelops them, and it seems that everything conspires to distance them from God. There are people who get married in the church because it's an ecclesiastical rite, others because it's a family tradition, or a requirement to fulfill or a social demand. All of these reasons contribute to underestimating the centrality of God in our lives and in our marriages.

These future spouses should be guided concerning the importance of building a strong spiritual relationship within their marriages. It's essential to affirm basic principles such as: we were created to be close to the Creator; marriage itself began with absolute and full communion with God; we must remain close to God and not come to Him only when we face a crisis. Another central principle in the life of faith of the newly married couple will be their involvement in the church and the development of their gifts. These aspects will transcend the marriage itself if their children are raised in the church environment, giving them an advantage in the development of their own Christian faith experience.

Course Duration

The duration of the course will vary depending on the material used and the available time of the couples and those who teach the course.

It's important that the course is not taken lightly and that a sufficient amount of time is set aside to discuss each topic. It's very valuable to give each session plenty of time so that each lesson is processed and assimilated by the couple. If the course takes place to close to the wedding date, the couple may not take advantage of it due to the demands and stress that the wedding often generates.

Sessions can be 60 or 90 minutes long, once a week, covering one topic per session. The number of sessions will depend on the number of topics/context to be covered. Between sessions, tasks such as reading, watching movies, taking tests, studying certain biblical passages, etc., can be assigned. Another option is to conduct a one or two day retreat — this is more convenient when there are several married couples who wish to take the course. The course could also be conducted in one, two or three weekends, depending on the time needed to cover all the topics/content.

Who Can Teach the Course?

The course can be taught or conducted by the pastor and his wife, or another experienced couple. It's not recommended that it be a newly married couple or a couple in the midst of an unresolved marital crisis. It's of the utmost importance that the couple teaching the course has a marriage that inspires with its example and that doesn't have a negative attitude that could negatively influence what is taught in the course. It must be a couple who is committed and who takes seriously the opportunity that the premarital course presents them to pray for the couples and accompany them in the process of entering marriage.

Premarital Course for Cohabitants

When we talk about premarital courses, we usually think of couples who have never been married or lived together as a couple before. However, the current reality is different. Now days, many people, both young and old, live together without getting married for many years. There are also those who get married by civil law without seeking God's blessing, others separate from their spouse and live with someone else, and others get a divorce and re-marry. It's also very common to encounter blended families,[2] couples who get married and who already have children that are attempting to create a new family together.

Many of these people meet the Lord and are coming to church. They have begun to strengthen their relationship with Christ, and Christ is moving them to make changes in their lives. Among these changes and rearrangements they begin to feel the desire to bring their lives and, if applicable, their newly combined families before the Lord. Marriage Ministries must encourage that decision and do everything in its power to ensure that the redemption in Jesus Christ also reaches these marriages. This means that they must be accepted as candidates for the premarital course, even if they already have a history of living together. From a pastoral perspective, let's not fail to take advantage of the opportunity to share the important topics of marriage from the biblical point of view to contribute to the reconstruction of life that God is doing in them (John 10:10; 2 Corinthians 5:17).

Experience shows that premarital courses make a significant difference in the marriages of the people who participate in them and this also applies to those who live together before getting married. Compared to those who have never been married before, the couples who have lived together/cohabitated have experiences that are very valid and interesting. Be aware of this as you approach the Word of God and see what it says.

An Opportunity to Contribute

We must take advantage of every opportunity that the Lord gives us to contribute, from the Word of God, to the construction of healthy marriages; in this sense, a premarital course is an excellent opportunity to do just that. With God's help we can grow closer to each couple and share the principles of God's Word in a different setting, through these classes, where we can build a relationship that gives support and journeys with these new marriages.

Instructions

Develop the curriculum for a premarital course.

_____
_____
_____
_____
_____
_____
_____
_____
_____
_____
_____
_____
_____
_____
_____
_____
_____
_____
_____
_____
_____
_____

Marriage Growth

Lesson 5

Marriage Growth

OBJECTIVES

- Understand the importance of creating an exclusive space for marriages in the local church.
- Recognize the importance of accompanying married couples in the development and growth of their relationship by providing practical tools that help strengthen the bonds of marriage.

MAIN IDEAS

- Marriage, from the divine perspective, is a living organism with a natural tendency toward growth.
- God created marriage so that man and woman may live their entire lives in exclusive unity like no other human relationship.
- Working to help marriages grow should take up much of our time and energy.
- When presenting the topics we must strive to put the Word of God into practice and thus provide relevant help to couples who are working on the growth of their relationship.

Introduction

In Genesis 2:24 God said: "...and they become one flesh". The obvious question that results from this divine mandate is; How is that possible? The apostle Paul himself acknowledges this as a great mystery (Ephesians 5:32). It is a mystery that we can discover, if we will intentionally incline ourselves to constant growth of the marriage bond.

Sometimes we hear that the verse "...and they become one flesh" refers to sexual union. Although this is true, it's equally true that this is a partial vision, since being "one flesh" or "becoming one being" has several points that imply continuous work in everyday life. This work is what we call marital growth.

For Your Whole Life

God's original plan for marriage was for your whole life. He didn't consider it a possibility to abandon the plan of being "one flesh". Marriage was designed to be a permanent commitment, for life. Jesus reaffirmed this original plan, that together with the Father and the Holy Spirit was conceived, when he said: "... what God has joined together, let no one separate."

> "Becoming one being" has several points that imply continuous work in everyday life.

Thinking about marriage from God's perspective means abandoning the possibility of separation and divorce. It means working committedly (day after day) to grow and strengthen the bond of marriage. It's interesting to see what was discovered by the American Values Coalition of the United States in a national report where it reveals that "two out of three adults who were unhappy in their marriages and avoided divorce, reported five years later that they were happily married".[1]

Along the same line of thought, Michele Weiner-Davis, a renowned American therapist, says that "studies show that the main causes that lead to divorce are not physical abuse or addiction but lack of communication, lack of affection and constant nagging... Actually I don't believe in 'saving marriages' but in ending the old one to start a new one with the same person".[2]

We must recognize that both marriage and divorce are for life. Therefore, Marriage Ministries cannot fail to assume marriage is for life; we must forget about divorce and commit ourselves to work towards the marital growth of those whom God allows us to shepherd.

Born to Grow

Many authors and scholars of marriage agree that marriage is a living organism and as such its natural tendency is to grow. In this natural process of growth, like human beings, marriage will go through different stages of development. These stages can be listed and named in different ways, but in general terms, we can refer to them as the following: (1) the couple knows each other, (2) they start a steady relationship, (3) they get married, (4) they start life together, (5) the first child is born, (6) they have a midlife crisis, (7) they become empty nesters, and (8) they enter retirement.

All stages of marriage are important, because the conflicts that arise will be impacted by the stage of development that the marriage is going through. Furthermore, at the different stages, each marriage has its own process to go through.

Each stage that a marriage goes through presents challenges and obstacles that offer unique opportunities for learning and growth.

Do you agree that marriage is for life?

What do you think about the statement: "We are not finished products"?

It's important to note here that each stage that a marriage goes through presents challenges and obstacles that offer unique opportunities for learning and growth. Understanding this is extremely important so that when the marriage naturally faces the situations that each stage brings, it does not despair. That way it will grow naturally and become stronger.

Marital Growth is the Key

Growth is a key word in married life. Just as human life is constantly growing, so is married life. We never stop, we are constantly changing and adjusting. It should be natural for us, but of course it doesn't come naturally within marriage. That's why Marriage Ministries is called to shepherd couples; to motivate, inspire, guide and accompany them in their growth.

Marriage Ministries works under the principle "we can always be better" since we can never consider ourselves perfect in our relationship and we will always have something new to learn. We are not a finished product, we can always grow and we can always overcome obstacles to reach a higher level of coexistence in married life.

This focus of our ministry will help us bring all married couples together. When we provide activities for married couples, the general thought is that those who should attend these activities are married couples with problems, those marriages that are "struggling". The result of this thinking is that marriages that are considered to be "good" don't participate, and those who know that their marriage is not going as it should don't attend because they don't want to give the appearance that they might be "struggling".

"We can always be better"! This must be our ministry focus. By promoting marital growth in this way, we will be able to avoid couples being singled out and judged; to naturally face the need to work constantly on the growth of our relationship; and to work together equally, each marriage growing from the stage in which it's in and moving to a higher level of satisfaction in their marriage.

Themes To Help With Growth

As for marriage, the topics to be discussed will be varied but recurrent, although from different approaches. Sometimes we can deal with several topics together since sometimes the treatment of one topic will involve others but from different perspectives. This will give us the opportunity to present the topics from different angles, thus helping in understanding them.

It's important that Marriage Ministries strives to bring the deep issues of marriage onto the field of practice. Move away from the masterful exposition and seek to share the themes so that the participating couples can take away something relevant to their reality and begin to put it into practice in their relationship. We must never lose sight of the fact that marriage was planned in heaven to be lived on earth.

Below, we present a list of topics, which without pretending to be complete, can help us when thinking about topics for activities within the framework of marital growth.

Communication

Verbal

Non-verbal

Active Listening

Differences Between Men and Women

Physical

Psychological

Emotional

Biblical Principles for Marriage

Equality

Unity

Complementary

Conflicts

They're Natural

How to Handle Them

Forgiveness

Finances

Budget

Expenses

Savings and Investments

The Extended Family

What does it mean to "leave father & mother"

Married (a house for two)

A place for family

Roles

What are they and how do the function?

Daughter, Son, Wife, Husband, Mom, Dad, Grandma, Grandpa . . .

Who does what?

Marital Sex Life

Love

Mutual Satisfaction

No Obligation or Right

Physical Health of Spouses

Healthy Food

Regular Exercise

Adequate Rest

Spiritual Health of Spouses

Personal Relationship with God

Studying the Word with My Spouse

Active Church Involvement

Time Management in Marriage

Order of Priorities

A Schedule

The Important and Urgent

Something Else To Keep In Mind

For a myriad of reasons, many couples find it difficult to admit that they need help. Therefore, it will be very rare for them to seek help from marriage counseling or therapy, with us or with other professionals. But, if marriage growth activities are well prepared and carried out in a practical way, we can significantly help these couples. We can contribute indirectly and anonymously, because in the development of each activity, people will be able to identify with the problems presented, self-assess themselves with the proposed exercises and games, reflect on the Word of God that is presented, and take for themselves those things that they consider valuable and that will help in their marriage.

Testimony

Some time ago, at a Retreat for married couples that we held, we were struggling with a married couple who had signed up for the event but due to the problems they had, they did not want to attend. This was a couple who had been married for many years who had a long history of unresolved conflicts. Previously they had expressed they were facing serious problems and suggested divorce several times.

One day before the Retreat began, at dawn they sent us a message saying that they were not going to attend and had made the decision to get a divorce. We prayed together and replied to their message, trying to make them understand that attending the event would benefit them a lot and that they should give themselves a chance. We fell asleep not knowing if they would attend or not.

The next day, they arrived. They immediately approached us and wanted to have a counseling session. During Retreats, the time is filled with different activities that are carefully planned and normally we don't take time for counseling. We encouraged them to participate in the activities while we tried to figure out when we could make time available for some counseling.

They participated in all the activities and never again approached us about a counseling session. At the end of the event, we told them that we were available and that we could take some time for the "pending" counseling session. It was then, holding hands and with smiles on their faces, that they told us: "It's no longer necessary. We weren't going to come because we had decided to get divorced... But by coming to the Retreat and participating in the activities we found a response to our situation. We are leaving with a lot of things that we have to change... but we're going to work on our relationship, we're not going to get divorced anymore."

Instructions

Pick a topic and get ready for the next Marriage Ministries activity.

_____
_____
_____
_____
_____
_____
_____
_____
_____
_____
_____
_____
_____
_____
_____
_____
_____
_____
_____
_____
_____

Marriages In Crisis

Lesson 6

Marriages In Crisis

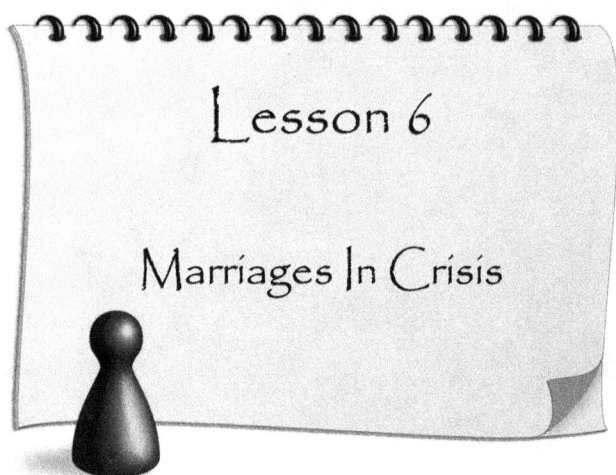

Introduction

We can say that all the work that we carry out as leaders, caring for others, has to do, in one way or another, with crisis prevention. In other words, it has to do with empowering people to cope with the different circumstances in life and avoid possible crisis. From deep analysis of the Word to the occasional small talk, to going through group Bible studies, Sunday School classes and personal discipleship classes, among others, space is provided with the intent to equip people with resources to face the various situations that arise, now and in each stage of their development. There is no doubt that this is so. There is a lot of effort put into providing these spaces, a great investment of resources, but we must admit that there are times when these goals are not met and both individuals and marriages face crises.

In regard to this, the apostle Paul allows us to understand our role in the community of faith. He says: "Praise be to the God and Father of our Lord Jesus Christ, the Father of compassion and the God of all comfort, who comforts us in all our troubles, so that we can comfort those in any trouble with the comfort we ourselves receive from God" 2 Corinthians 1:3-4 (NIV). We are helped so we can help. We are part of the solution. Our involvement is vital when a marriage faces a crisis.

> "He comforts us every time we have trouble, so when others have trouble, we can comfort them with the same comfort God gives us" 2 Corinthians 1:4 (NCV)

Definition of Crisis

According to the Merriam-Webster dictionary, a crisis is a "an emotionally significant event or radical change of status in a person's life."

OBJECTIVES

- Understand the meaning of a "marriage in crisis", its scope and how we can help.
- Understand that through proper crisis management, marriage relationships can strengthen and grow.

MAIN IDEAS

- Despite our efforts to prevent them, we should not be surprised when marriages face crises.
- A marriage crisis is one more opportunity for Marriage Ministries to make a significant contribution, offering a positive and hopeful approach so that the couple can adequately work through the crisis and grow in their relationship.
- Regardless of the crisis that a marriage is going through, Marriage Ministries must accompany the process in love and provide all the resources at its disposal to reach a solution.

Psychotherapist Howard Clinebell says "crisis occurs within people when their current activities aimed at solving problems are ineffective, thus allowing the tension of an unmet need to increase without ceasing".[1]

We can say that a marital crisis occurs when an unsustainable point is reached, where both parties cannot reach an agreement, and on many occasions, where time has passed without taking measures to resolve the situation.

We say a marriage is in crisis when a married couple reach a point in their marriage development in which they are overwhelmed by a situation that they cannot resolve together with the resources and abilities they have. They need help, external intervention, to face that crisis.

Here it's necessary to point out that not all problems, losses or tragedies will lead to a crisis. A loss is not a crisis in itself. The crisis consists of the inability that a couple has (with their own resources and abilities) to face the situation.

Negative Connotations of Crisis

The word "crisis" has been given a negative connotation. On repeated occasions we hear people refer to a crisis as something that will end those who face it. When talking about a marriage in crisis, most people are inclined to think that the relationship is about to end. This is because, often, when we refer to crisis, we associate it with loss or failure. Of course a crisis can include loss and failure, but not necessarily.

Here it's appropriate to mention that the word "crisis" in Greek means to separate or decide, resolve, interpret. It's also where the word "critical" comes from, which means analysis or study, and the word "criterion", which means proper reasoning. All of these Greek meanings lead us to think of a crisis as a crucial point in which we have to reflect, analyze and make decisions.

From a responsible leadership role and affirmed by the hope that God provides, when talking about a marriage crisis we need to do so with a positive perspective that conveys that it can be a positive experience if we handle it properly. It's here that Marriage Ministries will make its contribution, helping to train marriages to handle a crisis so that once they've properly worked on their relationship, they will be strong enough to face the coming crises and will even be able to help others.

Each Marriage Defines Crisis

When we talk about crisis we must bear in mind that it's not necessarily the same for everyone. We can say that there are

How would you define "crisis"?

events with universal characteristics from which the vast majority of people would enter into crisis. But when faced with other events, some marriages would go into crisis and others would not.

Each couple has their own way of living through the events that take place in their lives and therefore their own ways of dealing with them. While "getting fired from a job" for one married couple can be an event that brings them into a crisis, for another it can be the starting point of a new venture as a married couple. While for one couple "where they are going on vacation" may be the trigger of a crisis, for another it never will be. And while the notification of a traffic violation for one married couple can lead to a crisis, for another a lawsuit can be something that's even "normal".

Each marriage is unique and throughout life it creates its very own system which allows the couple to develop resources and skills to deal with the different events they experience. That's why we say that each marriage defines crisis.

Types of Crises

As we mentioned, crises are defined by each married couple, based on the way the couple handles a situation that is initiated by a triggering event. The psychiatrist Frank Pittman[2] who has studied crises in the family, classifies crises into four different types: developmental, circumstantial, structural and helplessness.

Developmental Crises. These are normal crises because they are part of the evolutionary process that a marriage naturally experiences in the different stages of its development. They are the transitions that occur from one stage to another, for example from dating to newlyweds, from newlyweds to parents and so on throughout their lives. The changes in each stage imply a series of modifications (roles, responsibilities, etc.) that we naturally want to resist when adapting to the new stage. These transitions, depending on each marriage and the resources and abilities of the couple, may or may not produce a crisis. In this regard, Norman Wright says that "most of these events can be seen coming on the horizon. The person can prepare for them by mentally imagining what they will be like, before they arrive."[3] Preparing for the next stage is nature's way of reducing stress, actively adapting to the new reality, and naturally growing the marriage. We call this a qualitative leap. This occurs when the marriage faces a crisis, works through it properly and learns from it.

Circumstantial Crises. These crises are brought about by those events that we don't expect and cannot prevent or even imagine, such as: an accident, an assault, a rape, an illness, death, abuse in all its forms, an economic catastrophe, a fire, a flood, a hurricane, among

What does it mean that crises are defined in every marriage?

Think of some events that are part of the development of a crisis.

many others. Some crises have the ability to affect the entire environment, for example a natural disaster that affects an entire community. On the other hand, others only affect us and our immediate environment, for example an accident or the death of a loved one. These events are not related to the natural development of marriage, and they are unexpected so they will naturally produce a crisis, although its magnitude will depend on the marriage.

> Crises are normal, they occur due to the developmental processes that a marriage naturally experiences in the different stages that it goes through to survive.

Structural Crises. These are not normal crises, although in marriages where they occur they seem to be. They result from internal issues that haven't been resolved and hinder the process of growth and development. They are the type of crisis that a marriage just "lives with" because, although there was an external triggering event, there is an internal force within the couple to avoid change. Family counselor Jorge Maldonado says: "families in perpetual crisis learn to flirt with disaster in order to avoid feelings of emptiness and despair. If you grow up feeling cold, depressed, without value or power, crises make you feel alive".[4] Generally, this type of crisis is associated with different types of addictions, violence, and different pathologies. They are more complex and sometimes require specialized care.

Helplessness Crises. These crises are associated with a specific situation, such as when one spouse is dependent and needs specialized care. When a couple or a family has a chronically ill person, a family member with mental illness, or someone with disabilities who needs constant care, the other family members sometimes feel like "prisoners", having to always be available for the ill person. For couples and families facing these crises, it's often a hard process to accept the reality of the situation as well as reorganize the marriage and family around the care of the ill person. The marriages and families that accept it and move forward take that qualitative leap in learning and move towards health. These crises tend to be long term and drain the very resources and skills that the members of the marriage and family have.

Finally, we must point out that since life is constantly changing, marriages may experience more than one type of crisis at the same time. In a way, it's normal for this to happen, since a crisis will not ask for permission from the previous crisis to begin nor will it wait for the current crisis to be worked through and the marriage to be "ready" to face another.

How do you think we can define what type of crisis a married couple is going through?

49

Forms of Intervention

Marriage Ministries can contribute significantly to the healthy growth of marriages. Previously we have referred to the fact that we can help indirectly by touching on different topics from different fronts: teaching, visiting, group and individual conversations, Bible study groups, different activities exclusively for couples that we prepare, among others. However, there will be marriages that will face crises that they cannot resolve and external intervention such as marriage counseling will be necessary. In these situations, "short-term crisis counseling can often be most helpful if it simply steers people away from inadequate responses and toward constructive confrontation with the crisis".[5]

This is where having developed a relationship of acceptance and trust with the married couples will be essential for them to feel comfortable to come to you for help. When, after making ourselves available, they are the ones who contact us so we're "50%" closer to the solution. Intervention or help in these cases does not mean going where we're not asked.

When the couple comes to us, we must listen to them with all our attention and patience, with objectivity, without judgment, asking pertinent questions to make sure that we clearly understand what they are facing and encourage self-reflection.

Once the crisis is defined, we must propose a solution strategy. It's important that we encourage the couple to understand that they, with dedication and work, can solve the crisis they're going through. At the same time and depending on the situation, we can make a referral to other professionals or so that they receive complementary care to ours.

Then we must establish concrete actions that they can take to work towards the solution. Remember that crises are a great opportunity for growth. So we must be intentional and celebrate progress, no matter how small. Sometimes one or both of the spouses will be overwhelmed and will want to quit/leave, at that moment we need to be the will they've lost and the renewed courage to continue (Galatians 6:2).

Next, we must identify the end of the crisis and when to end marriage counseling. There will always be marital problems, but a marriage must develop its own (good) ways of handling problems. Hence, it's essential to correctly define a crisis in order to work through it. That way we will avoid getting sidetracked from the crisis at hand and dealing with different problems as they arise.

In marriage counseling, whatever the crisis we deal with, the aspect that is essential and will be decisive in our intervention is love.

Qualitative Leap
(There was learning)

Life after a crisis has been worked through well

crisis

crisis

crisis

Life without crisis

crisis

crisis

Life after a crisis is badly or not at all worked through

crisis

crisis

crisis

crisis

Qualitative Leap
(There was learning)

Explain what "qualitative leap" means.

To Consider

Too often we find people who have developed an almost total dependency on a leader, pastor, or counselor. This is reflected in the fact that in whenever they face a difficult situation they turn to their "guide". Or there are those who say they cannot imagine living their life without the help and advice of this or that leader. It's worth mentioning here that this doesn't only occur in the context of the church, but it also occurs with health care professionals. "Therapists who become indispensable are dangerous."[6]

> In marriage counseling, dependency of the person(s) being counseled must be avoided at all costs.

In many cases this happens over time and it sometimes begins when people go through a crisis and received help. There are two factors that may cause this problem. (1) When the help was not produced by the marriage itself, but was given from the leader in the form of a formula that they had to apply. (2) When the intervention lasted beyond the necessary time. Anything that creates dependency must be avoided.

For Deeper Study:

Clinton, Tim and Hawkins, Ron. *Quick-Reference Guide to Biblical Counseling.* Grand Rapids, MI: Baker Books, 2009. 288 pages.

Clinton, Tim and Trent, John. *The Quick-Reference Guide to Marriage and Family Counseling.* Grand Rapids, MI: Baker Books, 2009. 304 pages.

Hegstrom, Paul. *Angry Men and the Women Who Love Them: Breaking the Cycle of Physical and Emotional Abuse.* Kansas City: Beacon Hill Press, 2004. 152 pages.

Time 20'

Instructions

How would you define "crisis" in your own words?

_____
_____
_____
_____

What types of crises can you name?

_____
_____
_____
_____
_____

Make a list of professionals, institutions, and organizations in your community that are qualified to intervene in different types of crises. It's important to have a list of reliable resources on hand that you can refer people to when their situation is beyond your capability to help.

_____
_____
_____
_____
_____
_____
_____
_____
_____
_____

Each Activity . . .

Lesson 7

Each Activity...

OBJECTIVE

- Show the important aspects that need to be taken into account when working on and completing a couples activity.

MAIN IDEA

- In the couples activities there are aspects that should not be taken lightly because the success of the activities and their continued use often depend on how seriously the activity is approached.

In every ministry, certain elements must be addressed when carrying out activities. Therefore, we've shared the following aspects that Marriage Ministries thinks are of vital importance that, in one way or another, will help in the development and continuity of the ministry.

Punctuality

Punctuality is a value that is greatly appreciated but, to tell the truth, in our environment it's highly undervalued. We need to understand its importance and return to making it a central aspect in our life and ministry.

Each meeting or activity should start at the established time. You should not wait for anyone, you should start with those who are present. This will set the tone for later meetings. In addition, those who arrive on time should be honored. You must take into account that for these meetings there will be married couples who must arrange with third parties to take care of their children and must return at the agreed upon time. So both the start time and the end time must be respected.

To encourage punctuality, if possible, you may want to announce that the couple who arrives first will be rewarded. The prize should not be something expensive, but simply something to motivate punctuality. A surprise punctuality award can also be given at the last meeting to the couple who attended all activities on time.

Depending on the type of activity or meeting, you may want to allow the first half hour to be a time to gather information from the attendees, take photos, among other things, generating a relaxed environment so that the couples can begin to interact, get acquainted and get to know each other. During this time, you can wait for everyone to arrive, providing coffee or soft drinks and snacks, fruit, or whatever is customary for your culture. You can also have recorded background music, or if possible, live music like someone playing the piano or a guitar.

Activities

In these activities, you should avoid having a single person speak for an entire hour. If a married couple is leading, it's key that both take part in the program and smoothly conduct the activity. One idea that works well in this regard is to divide the activity time into several short segments so that the program is more exciting. Another way to do this is to look for different formats for each meeting and thus avoid falling into a routine that bores the participants. You must always keep the element of surprise in mind, so that you can provide impactful activities and if you fill them with good content, the participants will have fun and learn something new to incorporate into their marriages.

Participation

It's important for people to participate during the activity. Different exercises should be conducted so that individual time is given to reflect, for spouses to discuss together, to work on a project together, etc. If any exercise is carried out in which the participation of a married couples is needed, always ask for a couple to volunteer and never force someone to participate. You must avoid making couples feel uncomfortable by asking them to share intimacies with the rest of the group. Marriage situations are confidential, intimate and of a private nature.

Be Careful! You must get to know the participants and if there are people who don't like to talk, you should not embarrass them by asking them to share if they don't want to because this may keep them from returning to the next activity. You must take the time, little by little, to get to know people.

Casual Atmosphere

This is an activity/meeting for married couples and as such it must be different from what is done in a worship service. There may be a prayer at the beginning and end and a topic to be discussed, but avoid presenting it like a church service. If you want to hold worship services for married couples, you can organize special worship services on different dates and include sermons and music that goes along with the theme, but meetings and other activities for married couples must be something totally different.

When we say informal meeting we mean a relaxed environment, where people can feel at home with a group of friends. This will help when people invite their non-Christian husbands or wives or friends (who are a couple) who don't yet know the Lord.

Why do you think it's difficult to do activities outside of the worship format?

When we say informal meeting we mean a relaxed environment, where people can feel at home with a group of friends.

Decorations

Decorations are very important. We have already mentioned that meetings for married couples are different than the worship services in which we celebrate regularly or the Sunday School or small groups classes we participate in. Therefore, you have to make an effort to provide a different concept for each activity. Remember the "element of surprise"!

The decorations will depend a lot on the physical space where you have the activity. Some spaces will need more decoration than others but it's important not to neglect this aspect. You can have the same basic decorations for each meeting, but on top of that incorporate some different elements each time you meet. You can also have a different decorations for each special occasion and this can go along with the theme that will be touched on in that activity, so that each element of the decoration communicates some aspect of the topic you'll discuss.

Decorations can include flowers, candles, dim lighting, hearts, motivational sayings, photos, etc. that will help create a pleasant and appropriate atmosphere for a married couples' activity.

You can look up web sites on the Internet where you will find endless ideas that will help you beautify each of the activities.

Music

Music is essential in almost any meeting, because it helps create a good atmosphere. So, in the activities for married couples we can't forget it. Of course, it should be music that encourages marriage relationships to grow stronger. Today we have a lot of Christian music with different rhythms and styles that talk about love in a marriage. But you can also search through secular music and pick out songs that encourage love within marriage. And if you're going to have live music, make sure it will be music that goes along with the activity.

Music videos can also be a good option if you have the equipment to show them. They are especially nice if you organize a special dinner or event, different from your usual activities.

Music can also help with the activities that you conduct with married couples or with a drama that you present. Fast, slow, suspenseful or reflective music can help you create an appropriate environment and attain better learning.

It's key to have one person assigned to this aspect of the ministry; to be in charge of everything related to music. They will look for the appropriate music, prepare it ahead of time and have it ready for the activity. They will also be responsible for the music throughout the activity, making sure the appropriate music is playing at the appropriate times during the activity.

Humor

We all like to have a good time, to laugh and enjoy the moment. This is life. However, many times we forget that humor can be an integrating element in our meetings. We get so involved in making sure the issues are treated seriously that we take a rigid and even tense approach to the issues and forget about the possibility of taking a relaxed approach when talking about the important issues of life. A fundamental way to deal with difficult topics is to use humor. Plato himself said that many times a joke helped where seriousness put up resistance. We can easily lose sight of the fact that cheerful teaching and cheerful learning can significantly increase the teaching-learning process.

A fundamental way to deal with difficult topics is to use humor.

This should encourage you to incorporate humor into your married couples activities. We're not saying that you should become clowns or impromptu comedians. Nothing like that. We're referring to humor that is well thought out and presented in a way that the listeners will naturally identify with the characters presented in a witty remark, joke or sketch. Humor as a natural and present element of everyday married life.

Social Time

As we have already mentioned, these are casual meetings, so it's a good idea to plan on having some social time to share. Having a social time will allow time for the married couples to get to know each other, and for you to talk with the married couples, and get to know them in an environment different from that of the church/worship setting. If there are new couples, a social time is especially helpful in getting to know them and possibly establishing a new friendship.

Social time can be at the beginning of your activity, at the end, or both. Greeting people with something to drink will be well accepted by couples who've been invited. Also, at the end of the activity, if a good atmosphere has been created, people will generally want to stay, talk and spend some relaxed time and pleasant conversation with friends. You can prepare coffee, soft drinks and sandwiches or desserts to share at the end. You can provide the refreshments, take turns with the participating couples or have each couple bring something like cookies or sandwiches to share. This will depend on the group. In the first meeting you can ask for help from the couples with whom you have more familiarity. Participation can be varied so that it doesn't become burdensome or limiting to the participants.

Photos

People always want to "capture the moment". Today, more than ever, that wish comes true through the use of our cellphones that have high quality cameras. It's important to keep this in mind. You can decorate a special area for married couples to take photos or make a frame for them to use to take the famous selfies.

Another option is to have a person assigned to take photos of different moments during the activity/meeting and of the entire group. This can later be used for promotion of the ministry and for the historical record of the ministry within the church, among other uses.

Children

It's important to understand that the activities for married couples is a space created just for "married couples". Just as there are activities for only men and for only women, this is an activity for only married couples. It's an exclusive time for them, therefore children cannot be permitted. Kids are kids, and they tend to require the full attention of their parents and often everyone around them. In an activity for married couples, children will get bored and won't let their parents enjoy the activity. Additionally, these meetings deal with topics that aren't appropriate for children.

We also recommend that child care NOT be provided for in the same building as the married couples meeting, because if the children cry or something happens to them, the children will want to be with their parents and the parents will want to be with children.

This position should be taken very seriously out of respect to all the couples who participate and take the trouble to leave their children with a care provider in order to spend some quality time together as a couple. If a married couple is not willing to leave their children with a trusted child care provider to attend the activity, it would be better for them not to attend, otherwise neither they nor the other couples will be able to take full advantage of the time together.

So, we must make an effort to make married couples understand the need to go out alone. Married couples need to be taught to enjoy time alone, without children around. Many couples, after the first child is born, never go out alone again, they take their children everywhere and lose their time together as spouses. Marriage Ministries must constantly encourage and help couples find ways to establish an weekly time away (date night) without their children. Encourage them to start by going out once a month, then increase it to twice a month until they reach a weekly time to get away. Over time, they will thank you!

Evaluation

It's good to consider conducting written evaluations. This can be done at the end of each activity, a cycle of activities or some particular activity that you want to evaluate. Far from being just another thing to do or opening the door to criticism, a well-conducted evaluation is a good tool to consider the feelings of the participants. It will help you to know what to continue to do and it will reinforce the positive aspects as well as show you what areas you need to improve on. The evaluations can be individual or as a couple, but they must always be anonymous, brief, written clearly and concisely, always leaving space for the participants' observations where they can expand on a particular aspect.

To complete the evaluations, allow some time during the activity, otherwise it will be difficult to get people to complete them as they will begin to withdraw and you will end up having very few evaluations. You can collect them several different ways: place a box in front of the room where the participants can deposit them when they've completed the evaluations; have someone pick them up as people finish them; place a well-marked box near the door for people to deposit them before leaving.

Promotion

We can provide the best of all activities, bring the most renowned speaker, rent the most appropriate room, but if we don't execute an adequate promotion strategy, failure is assured.

We live in a time where each person has a lot of options to choose from. We can't just assume that everyone will attend our activities. Whether we like it or not, our activities will be on the list of options that people have to choose from. Which will they participate in? Frequently, it'll be the activity whose promotion caught their attention.

So, for each activity that we're going to make available, we need to design an adequate promotion plan. For this, it's essential to study the people group that we are targeting and present the campaign in a timely manner to reach our desired results. Today, with technology we have lots of options that make it easier for us to promote and that significantly reduce costs. In any case, all means of advertising must be used to the maximum.

This would be a great task to delegate to a person who knows or is willing to be trained to do the promotional work for Marriage Ministries.

How do you think an evaluation of the activities would help?

Time 20'

Instructions

Individually or as a group, plan an activity for married couples taking into account the aforementioned aspects. Include as much detail as possible.

_____
_____
_____
_____
_____
_____
_____
_____
_____
_____
_____
_____
_____
_____
_____
_____
_____
_____
_____
_____
_____
_____
_____
_____
_____
_____

Activities

Lesson 8

Activities

OBJECTIVE

- Provide ideas of possible activities to do with married couples in order to enrich their relationships and help them in building healthy marriages.

MAIN IDEAS

- Develop different activities in order to fulfill the general purpose of Marriage Ministries.

- These activities must be carefully planned, taking into account the different specific objectives that Marriage Ministries pursues.

- Remember that we are always dealing with the whole person, so we must be careful to balance the topics discussed.

Possible Activities

When we talk about implementing activities, we tend to put the emphasis on the number of activities over other important aspects such as content. This approach can lead to exhaustion and end up adding more activities to the many that the church already has scheduled.

On the other hand, in Marriage Ministries we put a lot of emphasis on the time that couples must dedicate, so we must be very careful and meaningful with the emphasis we pursue. Thus, the activities must be carefully planned and maintain a healthy balance between them in order to bring growth to marriages.

Below is a suggested (not exhaustive) list of activities that can be implemented, but this does not mean that you need to do them all or that they should be done during the same time period.

Activities must be carefully planned.

Visitation

Marriage Ministry coordinators and their team must maintain a good and close relationship with all the married couples. They must take advantage of every opportunity to reach out to them. Set up informal meetings (a meal, have coffee, take a walk, etc.) to talk and get to know each couple. Take into account special dates such as birthdays and anniversaries to help you reach out and build relationships with these couples.

¿ What kinds of activities do you think can be implemented?

Dinners

It may be convenient to organize a dinner from time to time. This dinner must be special, and can be held in a restaurant, in a home, or in a room of the church building, decorated for the occasion, with individual tables for each couple and special music. The purpose of the dinner is to provide a space for married couples to have a special time for themselves. It can be a themed dinner, a speaker can be invited, a well-prepared drama or comedy can be presented, etc. The program must be varied and avoid the format of a worship service or normal church gathering. Something relaxed and entertaining will help in establishing relationships with married couples and in building a new paradigm in their married life.

Conferences

A marriage conference can be held at the church or in another location such as a community hall, a theater, or a restaurant, among others. One of the benefits of organizing marriage conferences is that they lend themselves to being open to the community and this opens up our circle of influence. One or more specialists can be invited to speak on topics of interest, you can have an book display along with other marriage resources, etc. A key aspect for the success of this type of activity is the promotion.

Recreational Activities

The purpose of these activities is to strengthen ties within marriages and also build friendships between the different participating married couples. For these activities, the most natural thing is to have them in the evening, however, they can take place at any time that is convenient. You can go bowling, share a meal, walk to a special place in the area, enjoy a show, etc. Day trips can be arranged for older couples and newlyweds, without children.

Evangelistic Campaigns

Evangelistic campaigns are an excellent opportunity to invite married couples who don't know the Lord and those who attend church but aren't attending Marriage Ministries activities. Also, they encourage those who have been attending Marriage Ministries activities to continue to participate. The campaign can be over a weekend, or for one or several nights during the week. The theme of the sermons for the campaigns will be salvation but from a marriage perspective, understanding that redemption in Christ reaches men and women in the marriage relationship.

Retreats

It's important to have retreats for married couples so they can get away together, without their children, and spend one or two nights away from home. Many couples, after returning from the honeymoon (and sometimes not even on the honeymoon), haven't gone out alone to spend quality time together as a married couple. This lack of time for their marriage gradually wears down the relationship, which in many cases leads to a fatal outcome.

Retreats are one of the most challenging activities to accomplish due to the economic cost involved and the family arrangements that each couple must make. In general, it's not an activity to do at the beginning of the ministry but after Marriage Ministries has been active for some time.

Film Forum

An activity that is appealing and can help us reflect on different topics is the film forum. This is not just about watching a movie, but it helps us think about and evaluate a specific topic. Many times, couples see themselves reflected in something that happens in the film and seek to improve or change it. If a film is going to be presented, the duration of the film must be taken into account, because it's important to show the film and then allow time for people to share what they gained or learned and have a brief closure to the activity.

When you organize a film forum there are two fundamental aspects: what do you want to achieve and what audiovisual medium will be used. Take time to select a good movie or series in which you can promote a theme or aspect of it. The participation of married couples and the discussion about the film is important. Those who run the film forum must know the film or series very well and be clear about the objective to be achieved.

As additional elements and depending on the customs of the area, you could create a theater like atmosphere, or create an atmosphere that goes along with the theme that will be discussed or the film that will be presented. You can even provide food and drinks or popcorn so that the participants feel at ease and are comfortable.

Small Group Study

These are just that, small and closed groups exclusively for married couples to study different aspects of marriage from the biblical point of view. It's not recommended to have more than five married couples per group. It's advisable to have groups of heterogeneous marriages in terms of ages, length of marriage, social class, professions and nationalities. Individual groups will decide the day, time and frequency of meeting together according to their availability. A very good resource to start with can be the "Making a Marriage" materials which consist of a guide for the leader and a book for each couple. These can be found on the MesoAmerica Regions' Discipleship

> Small group studies are closed groups (no more than five couples) exclusively for married couples where they can meet to study different aspects of marriage from a biblical point of view.

Ministries website: http://www.mesoamericaregion.org/en/ministries/Sunday-school-and-discipleship/discipleship-resources/.

Cell Groups

We speak of evangelistic cells or cell groups. These cell groups can meet almost anywhere, but they usually meet in a home. The homeowners are the hosts, another couple is the leader and another couple is the "Timothy", who will later become the couple who leads. The structure of the cell group meeting is usually: (1) Welcome, (2) Worship (Praise, Offering, Prayer and Testimony), (3) Message and (4) Mission (invite other married couples to participate). The recommendation is to have a weekly meeting that should not take more than 90 minutes. A simple way to do this is to take the message that was preached the previous Sunday and discuss the practical application, helping married couples live the Word they've received in the context of their marriage. The main objective of the cell groups is to reach new couples, so you should constantly be praying for new couples and inviting them to participate.

In the cell groups, in addition to contacting new couples and applying the Word of God to your marriage relationships, a close relationship of love, prayer and caring is generated among the participating couples; these relationships greatly impact the group.

Sunday School Classes

A class for married couples can be included in the types of Sunday School classes offered at your church. You can even have married couples classes that are separated by the number of years married. The thing to keep in mind when making these divisions is that the teacher of each class should help participating couples apply what they learn in class to reality. Otherwise it's just another Sunday School class and there's no reason at to have a class for married couples. Obviously, over the course of the year you will find some classes that apply better than others to marriages, but it will be the job of the teachers to help the participants find a way to apply the Word of God to their marriage relationship.

Book Club

This is an activity that can be attractive and very useful to married couples. It can be conducted in multiple ways, you can vary it until you find the best way to get the most out of it. A Book Club is basically defined as "a group of people who may or may not like to read but who are willing to read a book or parts of a book by a certain time and meet periodically to reflect together on what they have read."

The frequency, day and time, are aspects to be defined by the group, as well as the number of married couples to include and the type of books to read. This activity can serve several purposes, such as bringing the group together, having a social time, spending time together as a married couple (without kids), and expanding knowledge through reflection and discussion, among others. This website: http://www.mesoamericaregion.org/en/ministries/sunday-school-and-discipleship/discipleship-resources/ contains books that may be of interest to use to start a Book Club.

Family Week

This can be an annual activity. It can be planned during the week of May 15, going along with the "International Day of Families" instituted by the United Nations, or you can choose the day that's designated by the country or state where you live. A week dedicated to the family can be a magnificent time to affirm concepts, work on principles and values, open debates and share what the Word of God says about marriage and the family today. Depending on the location, during the day you can have different activities for all of the members of the family and workshops or other types of activities in the evenings. This is a great time to have a display of books and other marriage and family resources.

> May 15 is International Family Day. An excellent opportunity to plan an annual activity.

Celebration of Wedding Anniversaries

We naturally we celebrate birthdays but we don't tend to celebrate wedding anniversaries. The may be several reasons, but Marriage Ministries must support the marriages we work with and celebrating anniversaries is a great way to do so. One way you can do this is to announce the anniversary in a worship service and pray for the couple. Depending on various factors, this can be done during every service, once a month, or every so often. You can also announce the anniversaries in the church bulletin, on the bulletin board, on all social media groups associated with Marriage Ministries and your church. Something that is very well received by married couples is receiving an anniversary card from Marriage Ministries on the day of the anniversary. The goal is to reinforce marriage as God's creation and the basic unit of the family and society.

Special Dates

Special dates are specific days or weeks marked on the international calendar in order to promote, raise awareness and generate positive action for what is celebrated. Thus, we find several special dates during the year that, in one way or another, are related to the theme of marriage. We can take advantage of these dates to add value to and strengthen the marriage by promoting different types of activities. Additionally, we suggest looking for other dates on the calendars of your own countries that may be helpful for this purpose. Below we've suggested some special dates and given their origin in order to encourage you to take advantage of planning different activities for each of them:

February 14 – Valentine's Day. We've found several theories as to the origin of this special day, but probably the one that is closest to reality occurred in Rome in the third century, when Emperor Claudius II, by means of a decree, prohibited young men from marrying because he argued that single men were better soldiers than married men. Given this fact, a priest named Valentine continued to secretly conduct wedding ceremonies for young lovers, considering the decree to be unfair. When the emperor found out, he ordered Valentine imprisoned and executed on February 14, 270. Pope Gelasius I, in the year 498, was the one who declared February 14 as Valentine's Day, and for many centuries it was a religious holiday.

2nd Sunday of February – World Marriage Day. The origins trace back to 1981, in the city of Baton Rouge, Louisiana, United States, when a group of married couples petitioned the mayor, the Bishop and the governor of the state, to proclaim Valentine's Day as "We believe in Marriage Day". The event was well received and the idea of celebrating the day was presented to and adopted by the United States National Leadership of Worldwide Marriage Encounter. In 1982, 43 U.S. governors officially proclaimed the requested day. Then in 1983, the name was changed to "World Marriage Day". Since then, this day has been celebrated in various countries and in different ways, in which it seeks to honor the marriage union as the nucleus of the family and society.

What ways can you think of to celebrate wedding anniversaries in your local church?

April 13 – International Kiss Day. Even though it's not recognized as an official holiday, it seems like a good excuse to celebrate love through this (often neglected) demonstration of love: kissing. This popular celebration seems to have its origins in a record contest which took place in Pattaya, Thailand, in 2013, that was looking for the longest kiss. The prize went to a couple who kept their lips together for 58 hours, 35 minutes and 58 seconds. Along with earning the Guinness World Records title for longest kiss, the Thai couple also received a large cash prize and two diamond rings.

May 15 – International Family Day. On September 20, 1993, the United Nations (UN), named May 15 as the International Day of Families (http://www.un.org/en/observances/international-day-of-families). The international organization wishes to reinforce the importance that the international community places on the family. This day provides an opportunity to promote awareness of issues relating to families and to increase the knowledge of the social, economic and demographic processes affecting families.

In addition to International Family Day on May 15, some countries celebrate a national family day on other dates, such as Argentina (the third Sunday in October), Brazil (December 8), Paraguay (the fourth Sunday in April), Peru (the second Sunday in September) and Venezuela (November 15).

Time 15'

Create a year-long calendar scheduling some of the activities mentioned and/or activities that you want to plan, making sure to include valuable content that will help to strengthen marriages. Remember that you don't have to do an activity every month or do every activity. (You don't need to use all the space provided. Feel free to add space if you need to.)

Date	Activity	Purpose
_____	_____	_____
_____	_____	_____
_____	_____	_____
_____	_____	_____
_____	_____	_____
_____	_____	_____
_____	_____	_____
_____	_____	_____
_____	_____	_____
_____	_____	_____
_____	_____	_____
_____	_____	_____
_____	_____	_____
_____	_____	_____
_____	_____	_____
_____	_____	_____
_____	_____	_____

Notes and Bibliography

Lesson 1:

1- David Popenoe and Barbara Dafoe Whitehead, "The State of Our Unions: The Social Health of Marriage in America" The National Marriage Project, Rutgers University, 2001, p1.

2- Sobre Revoluciones Ocultas: La Familia en el Uruguay (On Hidden Revolutions: The Family in Uruguay), page 10. Document prepared by CEPAL (United Nations Economic Commission for Latin America and the Caribbean), Montevideo Office. http://www.cepal.org/publicaciones/xml/6/10566/LC-R141%20.pdf

3- Instituto Nacional de Estadística y Censo (INEC) (The National Institute of Statistics and Census[Ecuador]) http://www.ecuadorencifras.gob.ec/los-divorcios-crecieron-8345-en-diez-anos-en-ecuador/

4- George Barna, The Second Coming of the Church (Nashville: Word Publishing, 1998)

5- Source: https://noticias.gospelmais.com.br/40-mulheres-sofrem-violencia-domestica-evangelicas-86697.html ("40% of women who experience domestic violence are evangelicals" from GOSPEL News, Brazil)

6- Church of the Nazarene Manual 2017-2021, 340.2 page 176.

7- http://news.harvard.edu/gazette/story/2017/04/over-nearly-80-years-harvard-study-has-been-showing-how-to-live-a-healthy-and-happy-life/

Lesson 2:

1- The quote comes from the Preamble of the Constitution of the World Health Organization, which was adopted by the International Health Conference, held in New York from June 19 to July 22, 1946, signed on July 22, 1946 by the representatives of 61 States, and entered into force on April 7, 1948. The definition has not been modified since 1948. http://www.who.int/about/frequently-asked-questions

2- Ohani Center. (We are integral (whole) beings) http://www.ohanichile.com/somos-seres-integrales/

Lesson 3:

1- Serving in this capacity is entirely voluntary.

2- Reporting periods will be established by the local and/or District NDI Councils.

Lesson 4:

1- Carroll, J. S., & Doherty, W. J. (2003). Evaluating the effectiveness of premarital prevention programs: A meta-analytic review of outcome research. Family Relations, 52, 105-118: https://onlinelibrary.wiley.com/doi/abs/10.1111/j.1741-3729.2003.00105.x; Premarital education, marital quality, and marital stability: Findings from a large, random household survey. Journal of Family Psychology, 20(1), 117-126: http://psycnet.apa.org/record/2006-03561-013

2- According to Grosman and Martínez, the blended family is "the family structure originating from the marriage or de facto union of a couple, in which one or both of its members have children from a previous marriage or relationship." Grosman, C. and Martínez A. (2000) Blended families. Editorial University of Buenos Aires, Argentina.

Lesson 5:

1- Does Divorce Make People Happy? Findings from a Study of Unhappy Marriages. http://www.americanvalues.org/catalog/pdfs/does_divorce_make_people_happy.pdf

2- Su matrimonio siempre puede ser mejor (Olvídese del divorcio) [Your Marriage Can Always Be Better (Forget Divorce)]. Michele Weiner-Davis. Publisher Norma. Colombia, 2004. Page. 13.

Lesson 6:

1- Clinebell, Howard. Asesoramiento y cuidado pastoral. (Basic Types of Pastoral Care and Counseling) Published by Libros Desafío. USA, 1996.

2- Pittman, Frank. Momentos Decisivos: Tratamiento de Familias en Situaciones de Crisis (Turning Points: Treating Families in Transition and Crisis). Buenos Aires: Published by Paidos, 1990, pp. 29-43 [Spanish edition].

3- Wright, Norman. Como aconsejar en situaciones de crisis (How To Counsel in Crisis Situations). p 24.

4- Maldonado, Jorge. Crisis, pérdidas y consolación en la familia (Crisis, Loss and Consolation in the Family). Published by Libros Desafío, USA, 1999. p.37

5- Clinebell, Howard. Asesoramiento y cuidado pastoral (Basic Types of Pastoral Care and Counseling). Published by Libros Desafío. USA, 1996. p 184

6- Pittman, Frank. Crisis Familiares previsibles e imprevisibles (Predictable and Unpredictable Family Crises), p.366 (citado por Jorge Maldonado, Crisis, pérdidas y consolación en la familia. p.40 [quoted by Jorge Maldonado. Crisis, Loss and Consolation in the Family.]

www.ingramcontent.com/pod-product-compliance
Lightning Source LLC
Chambersburg PA
CBHW081225020426
42331CB00012B/3080